W9-CMJ-111

8/11

This book has been published in cooperation with Evans Publishing Group.

Published in the United States by
Amicus
P.O. Box 1329, Mankato, Minnesota 56002

Printed in China by New Era Printing Co.Ltd

Library of Congress Cataloging-in-Publication Data

Senker, Cath.
  Hospitality and catering careers/ by Cath Senker.
     p. cm. -- (In the workplace)
  Includes index.
  Summary: "Describes jobs in the hospitality, food, and catering business. Includes
information on hotel, restaurant, and catering jobs"--Provided by publisher.
  ISBN 978-1-60753-092-3 (library binding)
  1. Hospitality industry--Vocational guidance. I. Title.
  TX911.3.V62S46 2011
  647.94--dc22

                                                        2009045301

Editor and picture researcher: Patience Coster
Designer: Guy Callaby

The author would like to thank the following for their help in producing this book:
Jonathan Burcham; Mark Caldwell; Abi Cohen; Chris Edwardes; Margarita Fernandez; Tung
Mac; Mathieu Ouvrard; Tom Robinson; Kerry Trott; Andrew White; Kathy Murrer.

We are grateful to the following for permission to reproduce photographs: Alamy 6
(Danita Delimont), 7 (Peter Casolino), 11 (Andy Bishop), 13 (RIA Novosti), 14
(blickwinkel), 15 (Per Karlsson – BKWine.com), 16 (Peter Jordan), 18 (David Hancock), 20
(Peter Titmuss), 21 (brt PHOTO), 22 (Horizon International Images Limited), 23 (Jiri
Rezac), cover and 24 (Roger Bamber), 30 (Martin Thomas Photography), 31 (Ted Pink), 37
(WoodyStock), 38 (Jeff Greenberg), 42 (Directphoto.org), 43 (mediacolor's); Corbis 8
(Richard T. Nowitz), 12 (Lucas Jackson/Reuters), 17 (Hugh Sitton), 27 (Owen Franken), 28
(Juergen Wisckow), 29 (Becky Luigart-Stayner), 33 (Richard T. Nowitz),
35 (Jean-Marc Bernard/Realis Agence), 36 (Don Mason), 39 (Markus Moellenberg);
Getty Images 32 (AFP); iStockphoto 9, 10, 19, 25, 40, 41; TopFoto 26 (©The Image
Works), 34 (ImageWorks).

05 10
PO1568

9 8 7 6 5 4 3 2 1

IN THE
WORKPLACE

Hospitality
AND Catering
Careers

CATH SENKER

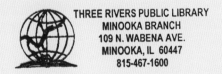

amicus
mankato, minnesota

Contents

The World of Hospitality and Catering   **6**

Chapter 1   **Working in the Hotel Trade**   **8**

Chapter 2   **Working in the Catering Trade**   **16**

Chapter 3   **Get Cooking: Kitchen Jobs**   **22**

Chapter 4   **At Your Service**   **30**

Chapter 5   **The Beverage Industry**   **38**

Further Information   **44**

Glossary   **45**

Index   **46**

The World of Hospitality and Catering

Hospitality and catering is a vast industry, with many job opportunities. In the United States, for example, more than 11 million people work in food preparation and service. If you decide on a career in this sector, you could find yourself working anywhere from a small, cozy neighborhood café to a large restaurant or a fancy five-star hotel. The locations are as varied as the jobs. Perhaps you'd like to work in your local town. If you feel adventurous, you could work abroad at a vacation resort, at a ski center, or even on board a cruise ship!

Waiters on a luxury cruise ship serve tea and dessert on board. Working on a cruise ship is a great way to see the world, although you have to be content to live in a small cabin for a long time.

WHICH JOB IS RIGHT FOR YOU?

If you are thinking about a job in the hospitality and catering industry, you'll need to decide on the area of work that will suit your talents. Are you good in the kitchen? Perhaps you'd like a job in catering. There are many kitchen jobs available. If you're a "people" person and a good communicator, a service job taking care of customers might be more up your alley. This could be in a restaurant or a hotel.

These bakers in a supermarket bakery in Connecticut are putting the finishing touches on some speciality pastries. This type of catering job will probably be available to you close to where you live.

There are opportunities for good organizers in hotels and catering. In fact, this is an industry where many people start at the bottom and work their way up to managerial jobs. Others set up their own hotels, bars, cafés, or restaurants and run their own business. Specialty jobs exist, too. For example, you could work in the beverage industry and become a wine expert or cellar technician.

Hospitality and catering are youthful industries. In the United States, for instance, 37 percent of the workforce is under the age of 24. Many people become managers by the time they are 30.

PERSONALITY AND SKILLS

For all hospitality and catering jobs, you'll need to be able to work as part of a team. It helps to have an outgoing personality, an ability to get along with all kinds of people, and a good sense of humor. For service jobs, professional presentation and a friendly nature are essential. Personality and common sense are more important than academic qualifications.

You'll need to be organized and good at multitasking. Hotels, restaurants, and cafés can be hectic places. You'll have to cope in a stressful environment, act effectively when problems arise, and stay calm in a crisis. Stamina is important; so is physical fitness—you'll probably be working long shifts on your feet.

TO WORK IN HOSPITALITY AND CATERING, YOU WILL NEED

●

"people" skills

●

an outgoing personality

●

the ability to multitask

HANDY HINT
Whatever stage you have reached in your education, find out which courses will help you in this field of work. If you plan to work in a place visited by large numbers of foreign tourists, you'll find it very useful to speak a foreign language.

Working in the Hotel Trade

Types of hotels vary enormously, from small boutique establishments to large budget hotels and five-star accommodations. Rooms range from the most basic bedrooms to luxury suites. Hotel jobs vary enormously, too, and serve every aspect of the guests' requirements. Keep in mind that working hours can be long and regularly may involve evening, night, or early morning shifts.

TO WORK AS A RECEPTIONIST, YOU WILL NEED

•

a friendly, welcoming personality

•

an ability to build a rapport with people quickly

•

plenty of energy

Many visitors book their hotel rooms online before they travel. This receptionist at a hotel in Moscow, Russia, checks the computer booking system when guests arrive.

RECEPTION STAFF

The reception staff in a hotel provides a crucial first impression to the visitors. In a small establishment, there may be just one person at the reception desk. Large hotels may have an entire concierge team, door attendants, and baggage porters. The door attendant welcomes guests and assists people who are less able.

Once guests are through the door, the receptionist checks their reservation and explains the facilities and rules. A porter then helps the visitors to find their room and brings their luggage. In a fine hotel, porters also run errands for guests, if requested. In a small hotel, they may take over the reception desk at night.

In addition to being friendly and welcoming, hotel receptionists require computer skills to manage computerized booking systems and should be able to work a telephone switchboard to answer calls. A good basic ability in math is important for preparing bills and exchanging foreign currency.

A hotel receptionist welcomes visitors with a smile. In large hotels, there will be a team of receptionists, with opportunities for promotion up to reception manager.

Jonathan: Head Concierge

"I started working in hotels as a porter and worked my way up to become head porter. After taking a hospitality management course, I took a job as deputy head concierge. I soon became head concierge. I'm head of front-of-house and manage 18 staff, including the doormen, concierge team, and hall porters. It took me six years to rise from being a porter to this position, which is pretty quick!

"It's a great job if you can strike up a rapport with people quickly. You should always be smiling and friendly—you can't have sulky faces in the hotel reception area.

"Each week I work four 12-hour shifts. My job is varied, and I'm always busy. I help guests with aspects of their hotel booking, from parking their cars and moving their luggage to recommending restaurants and arranging their flowers. Once I was even asked to help someone with a marriage proposal! Parking the cars is fun—one day you could be driving a Lamborghini, the next a Ferrari.

"As a good hotel, we receive great recognition in our town. Sometimes we are invited to restaurants or given free tickets to shows so that afterward we can recommend them to our guests. These perks help to make up for the long hours and low pay."

SERVICE STAFF

Service staff, such as room attendants, cleaners, and laundry workers, ensure the smooth running of the hotel. These jobs are often seasonal—workers are hired for the vacation season when the hotels are full. People usually work shifts, including evenings and weekends.

TO WORK AS A ROOM ATTENDANT, YOU WILL NEED

●
a flexible attitude
●
physical fitness
●
the ability to work quickly and neatly

ROOM ATTENDANT

After the guests leave, the room attendants come in with their cleaning supplies and vacuum cleaners to prepare the room for the next occupants. They have to work around the guests; some rooms may still be occupied and have "do not disturb" signs on the door. Room attendants work fast and in an organized fashion. First, they strip the beds and take away the towels. Then they thoroughly clean the bathroom, put out fresh towels, and replace the toiletries. In the bedroom, they put clean linens on the bed and empty the garbage cans. They dust and polish furniture and vacuum the carpet.

This hotel guest has chosen to eat breakfast in her room. Hotel rooms have to be kept spotlessly clean and neat, but good hotels ensure the staff also adds homey touches, like the flowers on this windowsill.

LAUNDRY WORKER

Hotels produce vast amounts of laundry. The laundry workers collect and sort the laundry; wash, dry, and iron it; and return the items afterward. With experience, a laundry worker can progress to become a laundry manager, supervising the other laundry workers and recruiting and training staff.

HOUSEKEEPER

The housekeeper is in charge of the service staff. The head housekeeper runs a team with assistant housekeepers, room attendants, and cleaners and is in charge of making sure all the bedrooms and public rooms in the hotel are clean and tidy. It's possible to work your way up from being a room attendant to a housekeeper, since the training is mostly on the job.

Much of the work revolves around the bedrooms. Once the room attendant has cleaned a room, the housekeeper inspects it before it is assigned to the next guest. The housekeeper also has to deal with any problems with the rooms, from broken lights and leaky faucets to flooded bathrooms.

It's worth knowing that in hotel work, you may start in one role and move into different jobs as they become available. It's good to be flexible and open to change to gain experience.

**MAIN TASKS:
HOUSEKEEPER**

●

recruiting and training staff

●

*managing the room attendants
and cleaners*

●

organizing staff schedules

●

*inspecting the rooms before
customers enter*

●

ordering supplies

*Room attendants clean the room
thoroughly after each occupant
has left.*

CATERING AND BAR STAFF

Most hotels have a restaurant and bar for their guests, so catering and bar staff are needed to run them (see chapters 2 and 3). The opening hours for hotel catering have to fit in with the guests. Your hotel might offer long, leisurely breakfasts until 11 a.m. or a late bar for night owls.

High-class hotels around the world now employ butlers. This butler is one of a special "white glove" team offering a personal service to guests at a plush hotel in New York.

SPECIALTY JOBS

Luxury hotels may offer their guests the special services of a butler. This is a job for people who want to work with VIPs. As a butler, you offer a personal service to your guests. You make sure that everything in the room is ready for them and greet them on arrival. You assist them with their luggage and are on call to attend to any special requirements. For this job, you need to be available for long hours and dress professionally at all times.

To be a butler, you have to be able to get along with all kinds of people, as well as be organized, trustworthy, and dependable. It's important to remain calm and polite at all times, whatever the demands of your guests. To apply for this job, you should already have experience in the hotel and catering industry. It's useful to have knowledge of fine dining and formal service in a high-class restaurant or hotel.

Chefs prepare the tables for a classy banquet in Moscow, Russia. To organize a complex event like a banquet, you need long experience in the hospitality industry.

MAIN TASKS: CONFERENCE MANAGER

● *finding a venue*
● *organizing the schedule*
● *arranging the catering*
● *taking reservations*
● *recruiting staff*
● *managing the budget*

Hotels are often the venues for conferences and special occasions, such as weddings. If you're a good organizer, how about training to be a conference and banquet manager? Organizing an event involves a range of tasks. You have to find a venue, discuss the client's requirements (including the budget), take the reservations, arrange the catering, and organize the schedule for the event. You recruit staff to run the event and deal with last-minute changes and problems. You need a calm personality and the ability to multitask.

TOP JOBS

With several years of experience in hotel jobs, you could be ready for a senior management post. In large hotels, there's a management team. The food services manager is in charge of buying all the food and beverages and may also plan the menus. There may also be an accommodation services manager.

Smaller and medium-size hotels may have one hotel manager or a management couple. If there's a couple, usually one person is in charge of the housekeeping and the other runs the kitchen. Running a hotel is a vocation—you'll have little free time away from the hotel.

FINDING A JOB: CONFERENCE MANAGER
For this job, you need experience in a junior role, such as serving drinks at events. You'll start off as an assistant under the supervision of a manager and will learn on the job. A degree in event management is useful, too.

To reach a senior position in the hotel trade, you'll need training as well as experience—for example, in management skills. Knowledge of hospitality law is crucial, too. You'll need technology and communication skills to cope with the administration of the business, and knowledge of accounting to organize the finances. You should also be competent in the area of human resources to manage your staff. If you work for a large hotel chain, you can choose to specialize in any of these fields. For instance, you could become a human resources manager.

An alternative to working your way up through the ranks is to study for a relevant degree, for instance, in hotel management or business. Then you could enter the industry through internships or other training programs.

STAYING AHEAD OF THE GAME

Even after you have a job, you'll need to keep up-to-date with the constant changes in the hotel industry. For example, many hotel managers today are making efforts to reduce the carbon emissions of their businesses. They ask guests to put towels out to be washed only if they are dirty (rather than having clean towels provided each day). This reduces the amount of laundry, saves water and electricity, and keeps down costs.

WHERE WILL I BE?
Most people start out in the hotel trade in an entry-level job and work their way up. With several years of experience, you could set up your own hotel. Alternatively, you could work for a large hotel chain, which will provide you with a clear career structure. You could end up managing big hotels.

This is a laundry room in a large hotel. If asked, many guests are happy to use their towels and bed linens more than once. This cuts down the amount of laundering and is better for the environment.

This couple co-owns a restaurant in Buenos Aires, Argentina. Co-owning is a good way to share the work and responsibility of a business while still having control over your working life.

Chris and Amanda: Hotel Managers

"My wife and I have been running a boutique hotel with 12 bedrooms for eight years. I've been in the hotel industry for more than 30 years. I started out in bar work when I was 18 and then worked in a restaurant for two years. I tried out all the jobs—in the bar, kitchen, and front-of-house. Then I met my wife, Amanda, who is an interior designer. We wanted to combine our skills and set up a business, so we decided to run a hotel. Amanda designed all the rooms individually, and I set up the restaurant.

"We employ bar staff, waiters, kitchen staff, room attendants, and a receptionist. I'm responsible for the day-to-day management of the hotel, doing all the administration, billing, and accounting. In the evening, I act as the maître d' in the restaurant, welcoming guests and bringing them drinks and menus.

"We have lovely customers, lovely staff, and a great atmosphere in the hotel. But it's hard to run a small business. I'd advise anyone to think seriously before committing to this career. You need to be passionate about the hotel business and prepared to be 100 percent hands-on, doing whatever needs doing. Even then, it's still tough!"

Working in the Catering Trade

Catering involves making and serving meals for people. It may mean providing lunch to hundreds of employees in workplace cafeterias or to small numbers in little cafés and restaurants. There are also catering services for people on the move.

FOOD SERVICE MANAGEMENT

A large part of the catering market is food service management (FSM), or contract catering. Food service companies sign a contract to provide the catering service for an establishment. This can be in the commercial sector, making food to sell for profit in workplaces, hotels, fitness centers, and restaurants. FSM also provides catering services for the nonprofit sector, for example, in hospitals, schools, and prisons.

Sometimes, food is cooked at a central location and transported to the institutions under the contract. Hospital catering is often done like this. The company and its hospital clients negotiate the food requirements. They discuss nutritional content—good food can help patients to recover. The company may provide dishes to cater for special diets, such as vegetarian or halal food. The food is cooked by a food service company and frozen to take to the hospital. The in-house caterers simply reheat the dishes, and the food is served in the hospital. This is a cook-chill catering system. The food may also be cooked in a catering unit on the premises, following the food service company's specifications.

Catering staff prepare airline meals at Heathrow Airport near London, England.

A REGULAR JOB

If you work for a food service company, you are told exactly how to prepare the food with approved recipes. You have to be meticulous about hygiene and health and safety to ensure that the food is safe to eat. It is less creative than working for an independent eatery. On the plus side, you will usually work regular daytime hours, and the job is generally less tiring.

TO WORK AS A CONTRACT CATERER, YOU WILL NEED
●
math skills
●
a knowledge of food
●
problem-solving abilities

Mark: Cafeteria Chef

"I've been working in a hospital [cafeteria] for 13 years, serving meals to staff and visitors. I started out in a hospitality and catering course at [technical school], where I learned the whole range of catering skills, including main kitchen, desserts, and silver service. As part of the course, I did work experience, and then I found a job at the hospital. My first job was taking around a sandwich [cart].

"I worked my way up and have been a chef for seven years. Every day, I cook the breakfasts and then prepare the lunches. We usually serve 200 to 300 people. I choose the menu. My favorite dishes are meat meals, such as beef stew and lasagna. I'm not so keen on desserts! The menu is limited because we just have two huge ovens rather than gas [ranges]; originally the meals were brought in frozen from a large company and simply reheated. The ingredients we can use are limited, too. For example, since it's a hospital, we can't cook with alcohol.

"The working hours are good, though. I work from 6 a.m. to 2 p.m., five days a week. It's far less stressful than working in a normal restaurant."

A chef prepares vegetables. If you're looking for a steady job in catering, then working as a chef in a hospital cafeteria might suit you. Most of your training will be on the job.

Flight attendants serve refreshments in the business-class cabin of an aircraft. The attendants have to be knowledgeable about the food they are serving, and some become wine stewards.

HANDY HINT

A marine catering job provides a fantastic opportunity for travel. You will learn to cook high-quality food, so your experience may lead to excellent jobs back on dry land afterward.

FOOD ON THE GO

Another area is catering for people on the move. Whether you're traveling by train, bus, or plane, the chances are you'll want some refreshments during your journey. Transportation catering often uses catering systems.

For example, food for airline passengers is prepared on the ground by chefs in large kitchens. It is packaged up and loaded onto the aircraft. During the flight, the flight attendants heat up the hot dishes and assemble the food trays. They add the final touches, such as preparing fresh salads for first-class passengers. The food is served as attractively as possible, given the lack of space on board.

Marine catering involves more exciting cooking jobs. For sea travelers, dinner is the highlight of the day. Providing a varied and interesting menu is a job that requires flair and imagination.

SCHOOL LUNCHES

If you'd rather have a job on solid ground, and you enjoy working with children, then a career in a school setting could be for you. In a small elementary school, there may be just two workers in the kitchen: a head and an assistant. In a large high school, there will be a team of kitchen assistants, supervised by a head cook.

Kerry: Elementary School Cook

"I work as a kitchen assistant in a large [elementary] school. There are four of us working in the kitchen. Every day we serve around 120 school lunches. I didn't need any particular qualifications— I trained on the job. I had to take courses and pass exams in health and safety and food hygiene.

"I start work at 10:45 a.m. By this time, the supervisor and two other assistants have already prepared the vegetables, the main dishes, and the desserts. In our school, all the food is freshly cooked every day. I [help prepare the hot meals], and prepare the salads. We set out the chairs and tables in the [cafeteria], and then lunch begins.

Children get their lunch at a school cafeteria. The government sets nutritional standards to make sure that schools serve healthy food.

"Afterward we clear away the furniture, wash up, and clean the kitchen thoroughly. I finish at 2 p.m.

"For me, there are several advantages to the job. I have two children, so I can work while they're at school. If you want to progress in your career, you can work your way up and become head of the kitchen.

"The downside is the pay, which is quite low. But if the hours suit [you] and you enjoy working with children, it's worthwhile. The kids really appreciate us—they make us such lovely cards at Christmas!"

TOP JOB: CATERING MANAGEMENT

FSM offers many management opportunities. As caterers sign new contracts to provide food to more establishments, they need more managers to work with the new clients. In comparison with restaurant work, FSM offers the advantages of regular daytime hours and five days of work a week for a good salary. Excellent opportunities exist for promotion. There are challenges, too. Contract caterers need to be aware of changing demands in the food market—for example, many customers today prefer to eat foods that are fresh, locally sourced, and ethically produced.

FINDING A JOB: CATERING MANAGER

You can gain experience in the catering industry and work your way up to a management job. Alternatively, you can study for a degree or other high-level qualification in a relevant subject and join through a training program.

Meals from a food service company are loaded onto an aircraft from a catering truck. The catering manager works with the airline to ensure that the correct refreshments are provided at the right time.

These trainees at a contract catering company are demonstrating their food preparation skills. They will need to meet high standards to qualify for top catering jobs.

MAIN TASKS: CATERING MANAGER

planning menus

organizing staff schedules

making sure food and health safety rules are followed

ordering supplies and managing the stock

recruiting and training staff

keeping to a budget

SCHOOL CATERING MANAGER
A contract caterer often provides school meals for a district. The meals are cooked centrally in one place using a catering system and then delivered to the local schools. A catering manager is in charge of the process. The manager needs to balance children's tastes, parents' views, and teachers' views, and consider the nutritional value of the meals.

WHAT DOES THE JOB INVOLVE?
Whether they work in a school, conference center, daycare center or college residence hall, all catering managers need a range of similar skills. They must be excellent administrators, capable of overseeing budgeting, the maintenance of kitchen equipment, and the furnishing and decorating of cafeterias. You'll also need computer as well as management skills. Unless you work in a small institution, you'll probably never do any cooking yourself—although experience as a chef is a valuable asset. After a few years as a catering manager, you may take on more responsibilities as a director of catering, in charge of more than one site.

WHERE WILL I BE?
A wonderful aspect of this industry is that you will gain transferable skills. As a catering manager, you can move between hotels, cafés, restaurants, bars, and tourist attractions.

Get Cooking: Kitchen Jobs

A career in food preparation offers many possibilities. You could work in the kitchen of a fast-food outlet or a fancy hotel restaurant. Your tasks will depend on the cuisine of the establishment—you could be cooking food from almost anywhere in the world!

These chefs prepare fresh ingredients to cook Chinese food, which is popular around the world. Experience in Chinese cooking techniques, which include stir-frying, grilling, deep-frying, and baking, is helpful for any budding young chef.

A BUSY LIFE

Kitchens are busy, hot, and noisy places to work, and you'll be on your feet most of the time. At the end of a shift, you may feel drained, both mentally and physically. Yet a kitchen can be a very sociable place to work. You work long hours—sometimes up to 16 hours a day—with your team, so you get to know one another really well. Kitchen workers often socialize together after they have finished their shifts.

CUTTING AND CHOPPING

The entry-level jobs are kitchen assistant and busser. As kitchen assistant, you'll be responsible for basic food preparation. You'll chop vegetables and learn to use equipment such as mixers and other kitchen machines. You'll find out how to cut meat correctly and how to bone and skin fish. If you're working in a kitchen that caters to special diets, such as for Jewish people, vegetarians, or vegans, you'll learn how to meet these requirements. You may cook some simple dishes, especially if you work in a small kitchen. This might include making sandwiches, toast, salads, and soups, and preparing the drinks.

HANDY HINT

People from different ethnic groups tend to run cafés and restaurants that provide food from their country of origin. They will, however, still employ workers with different ethnic backgrounds. If you're considering a career in cooking, it's worth gaining experience cooking various kinds of cuisine.

CLEANING AND TIDYING

As part of your job, you'll wash dishes, keep the kitchen clean, and unload deliveries. It's essential to learn about health and safety. Kitchens are dangerous places, full of sharp equipment, hot ovens, and busy people. Food hygiene is crucial. Special antibacterial products are used to keep surfaces clean. You need to be spotless, too, wearing a fresh, clean uniform every day.

A kitchen porter helps to keep the kitchen clean and tidy; some of the jobs are similar to those of an assistant. Porters unload deliveries, clean the kitchen, load and unload dishwashers, clean floors, and dispose of waste.

Kitchen assistants have to wash large pieces of equipment by hand.

**MAIN TASKS:
KITCHEN ASSISTANT**

preparing meat, fish, and vegetables

making simple dishes

operating dishwashers

cleaning pots and equipment

cleaning the kitchen

unloading and storing food supplies

FINDING A JOB: KITCHEN ASSISTANT/PORTER
You don't need experience to become a kitchen assistant or porter, although an interest in food and catering will help. A large proportion of jobs are seasonal or casual—workers are hired to cover busy times, for example, summer or other holidays. This is a good time to get a foot in the door.

COOK YOUR WAY TO THE TOP

On the next level up from kitchen assistants and porters are the chefs. There are several different ranks of chef, each requiring more experience. They range from an apprentice chef up to the head chef, who is in charge of the whole kitchen (see pages 26–27). A small kitchen may have just one chef and an assistant. A large kitchen is divided into sections for making different kinds of food, such as fish, meat, and vegetables.

COMMIS CHEF

This is the apprentice chef level. As a commis chef, you'll work in each section of the kitchen to gain experience. You'll learn how to make sauces and desserts and how to prepare meat and fish.

CHEF DE PARTIE

This means "head of a section of the kitchen." Depending on the kitchen, you could be in charge of all the grilled foods, the vegetables, or the cold foods.

SOUS CHEF

The next level of chef involves management responsibilities. The sous chef stands in for the chef if he or she is not there. Your job includes training the junior staff and helping to plan menus. You'll be checking that staff stick to health, safety, and hygiene regulations at all times.

**FINDING A JOB:
COMMIS CHEF**
Set your sights high! Apply to the kitchens of the most famous chefs for a placement as a trainee. If you are lucky enough to find an opening there, you will receive the best training and can work your way up.

This student is learning to make pastry. Apprentice chefs can specialize in a particular area, such as confectionery (making candy) or patisserie (making cakes).

A chef checks the orders. At busy times, the kitchen can become very hectic, and it's important to keep a cool head.

Tom: Commis Chef

"I started out as a cook in a pub. I learned all aspects of the job: kitchen, bar, and front-of-house. I did work-based training in kitchen work; this involved learning which boards and knives to use and finding out about health and safety.

"I recently found a job as a commis chef in a Latin American restaurant. I'm being trained to cook main meals on the range, such as enchiladas and chimichangas, as well as making [appetizers] and desserts. It's great to learn new styles of cooking. The restaurant is part of a small chain. The company offers structured career development and pays for my training.

"It's a really satisfying job—the customers enjoy their meals and leave with smiles on their faces. It's far better than working nine to five in an office! The hours are long, though. On a Friday, I work a 16-hour shift, so I can't go out that evening with my girlfriend. I do like having a weekday off, though—it's quiet in town.

"To become a chef, you must be passionate about cooking. If you are, then my advice is to take a junior kitchen job. If you stick with it, you'll get trained and will soon be rewarded with a promotion."

TOP JOB: HEAD CHEF

For people with several years of experience in a kitchen, there are good management opportunities. The head chef manages the team of chefs in a kitchen and is responsible for all the cooking. In a small kitchen, you'll be doing the cooking yourself, perhaps with some assistants, as well as helping to serve and clean up. In a large establishment, you'll be supervising all the other chefs.

If you work in an independent restaurant, you are free to create your own menu. Chefs working for a chain of restaurants have to follow the menu established by the company. Today, many restaurant owners think carefully about where to source their ingredients. There has been a move toward sourcing locally produced and organic ingredients. As head chef, you need to take these trends into consideration.

As well as being a creative cook, you'll require many other qualities and skills. You'll need a strong personality to be able to recruit, train, and manage the kitchen team. There are organizational tasks, too. You'll be in charge of ordering the kitchen supplies, arranging deliveries, and taking inventory. Computer skills are necessary for these jobs and to help you plan the staff schedules. A head for figures is useful for controlling the budget.

A chef cooks shrimp at a high-class hotel in Canada. Chefs have to prepare high-quality meals quickly and are on their feet most of the time.

MAIN TASKS: HEAD CHEF
●
creating high-quality food
●
managing the budget for the kitchen
●
controlling food inventory
●
ensuring high standards of hygiene in the kitchen
●
recruiting and training staff
●
organizing the staff schedule

KITCHEN SUPERVISOR

To become a kitchen supervisor, managing all the chefs and other kitchen workers, you need to be a trained and experienced chef. You'll check food quality and delegate tasks to the staff. Part of the work is office-based, doing administrative tasks such as ordering supplies, keeping accounts, and updating records of staff, suppliers, and food orders. You need a high level of management and computer skills.

WHERE WILL I BE?

There is a long career ladder in kitchen work. If you are prepared to stay in the industry for several years, there are good chances of promotion. A kitchen assistant or porter can expect to rise gradually through the ranks to become a chef. To speed up the process, you can attend a culinary program— either a four-year program at a culinary school or a two-year program at a technical college.

A chef in a Monte Carlo, Monaco, restaurant tastes a dish prepared by his sous chefs. Sampling the food is an important task for head chefs and kitchen supervisors.

BUTCHER, BAKER, CONFECTIONERY MAKER

If you'd like to specialize in one area of food preparation, why not consider working as a butcher, baker, or confectioner? Once you have experience, you may be able to set up your own small business.

TO BE A CONFECTIONER, YOU WILL NEED

●

excellent hand-eye coordination

●

patience

●

the ability to work well as part of a team

BUTCHER

Most butchers work in retail, preparing meat and selling it to customers. Others work in wholesale; they take animal carcasses from abattoirs and prepare cuts of meat for use in restaurants and hotels. This is not a job for the squeamish! Animal carcasses are heavy and messy to work with. You'll need to be physically fit to lift them and be able to use specialized cutting equipment.

BAKER

Bakers work in large industrial bakeries, in-store supermarket bakeries, and small artisan bakeries, producing bread, cakes, and cookies. At a large industrial bakery, all the processes are automated, so you'll be operating machinery. An in-store bakery has some machinery, for example, to slice bread, but you'll do some of the work by hand. At an artisan bakery, you'll make a variety of products from start to finish: You'll weigh out the ingredients, make dough, bake the products, and then decorate and wrap them to be ready for sale.

CONFECTIONER

Have you got a sweet tooth? If so, this could be your perfect job. Confectioners make candies and chocolate. Sugar confectioners make candies, while chocolatiers hand-craft high-quality specialty chocolates, such as Easter eggs and chocolate assortments. You'll use special machinery to produce chocolate with the right flavor and texture, to mold it into shapes, and to mix the fillings. You need a steady hand for painting detailed designs, such as the features on a chocolate bunny.

A baker adds decorations to fancy cakes. This job requires careful attention to detail, good concentration, and a steady hand.

This cheesecake is decorated with fresh fruit. High standards of food presentation are essential in the bakery business.

Abi and Yoav: Bakery Entrepreneurs

"Yoav and I have always enjoyed cooking. Yoav has a degree in ceramics—his artistic ability helps with cake decorating.

"We developed our business from our own home baking, selling our cakes to local shops and restaurants. We specialize in cakes for special diets, such as gluten-free products. Our most popular lines are vegan carrot cake and Lebanese cheesecake with rosewater and orange-flower water—delicious! We now employ three other people to help make the cakes.

"On a typical day, we start making deliveries at 7 A.M. Beginning at 10 A.M. I have errands to run, such as going to the bank and picking up supplies for the bakery. I also spend about three hours in the office, doing invoices and other administrative tasks. Then I help to decorate the cakes and check [that] they meet our high standards. Sometimes I meet new customers in the afternoon. I usually finish work between 4 and 6 P.M.

"Recently, we started baking bread to expand the business. We invested in new equipment and employed two bakers who work overnight from 8 P.M. till 6 A.M.

"In this job, you have to be prepared to put in long hours. But when it's your own business, you don't mind."

At Your Service

On the other side of the kitchen door are the people who serve the food. Food service can range from one person working at the counter of a tiny café to a team of silver-service waiters in a high-class restaurant.

LARGE OR SMALL?

If you're considering a service job, think about whether you'd like to work for a large company or a small business. In a large company, there will be a career structure, with opportunities to rise to senior positions. In a small establishment, there will be less structure, but you may be able to learn about all aspects of the business through working closely with the managers. There are advantages to working in both types of business.

To start out, you could find a job as a waiter or waitress. In this job, you clean and prepare tables and welcome customers. You take their orders, bring their food, and clear the table afterward. At busy times, you will be rushed off your feet, but your working environment may be more pleasant than in the hot, noisy kitchen.

You don't need any special training to start out—but personality is crucial. In a restaurant, the service is almost as important as the food itself, so you need to be cheerful, friendly, and polite at all times. When the restaurant is full, you need to work fast while keeping track of everyone's orders. It helps to have a good memory—you'll meet many people, and it's useful to remember regular customers.

TO BE A WAITER OR WAITRESS, YOU WILL NEED

●

a clean, professional appearance

●

an outgoing personality

●

the ability to work quickly

A waitress serves coffee at an outdoor café in an Italian city. Many people start their catering careers as waiters or waitresses.

A waitress serves pizza at a New York pizzeria. Waiters and waitresses may work long hours.

Margarita: Waitress in a Pizza Restaurant

"I've been working as a waitress at a pizza chain restaurant for a year. I have eight years of experience as a waitress.

"I work eight-hour daytime shifts. I set up the restaurant, making sure the tables are ready and that we have enough Parmesan cheese, [crushed red pepper], and olive oil prepared. Then we serve lunch. It's a popular restaurant, and it gets pretty busy.

"This job suits me because I love Italian food. My husband is Italian— I speak the language and am knowledgeable about the cuisine. I often advise customers on the menu. It's a sociable job, too. I enjoy meeting lots of people, and the staff are friendly.

"It can be stressful at busy times, though, especially if customers complain about having to wait for their meal. Also, we have to cope with 'mystery diners.' The company sends people to eat in the restaurant to check if we're providing good service. We never know when this will happen!

"On balance, I think that being a waitress is a good job when you're young. You can travel and work wherever you go. But I don't want to do it forever. In a few years, I'd love to open up my own little Italian café."

FAST FOOD

Fast food is a huge part of the catering industry, ranging from international pizza and burger chains to small independent takeout restaurants. Fast-food restaurants serve many types of food: Mexican, Indian, and Chinese are some of the most popular.

HANDY HINT
Fast-food service jobs are usually part time and based on shifts. If you're a student, a flexible job like this can fit in well with your studies.

Customers wait for their orders at a Lebanese fast-food outlet in Dubai that offers shawarma— meat from a spit served in pita bread with salad and sauces.

FAST-FOOD SERVER

As a fast-food server, you take orders and serve meals and snacks. You mostly work behind the counter, assembling the orders and packing up the food. You have to be good at basic math to take payments from customers. In smaller establishments, you may do some simple cooking, too. There may also be jobs delivering takeout food to customers.

Working in the fast-food industry has some advantages. You'll receive useful training in health and safety, food safety, and hygiene. You may attend courses to learn customer service skills and basic food preparation. If you have the opportunity to cook as well as to serve food, you'll gain valuable experience. In this industry, it's relatively easy to progress to management level even at a young age—you can become a supervisor or even a store manager. Big companies offer a management training program to enthusiastic employees.

This Japanese bar serves sushi dishes—rice served with vegetables and seafood.

MAIN TASKS: FAST-FOOD SERVER

●
taking orders

●
assembling orders and providing drinks

●
taking customer payments

●
ensuring the service area is well stocked, for example, with condiments

●
keeping the service area and restaurant clean

UNDER PRESSURE

One disadvantage of the job is the pressure—you have to serve people fast. You may be instructed to serve a customer every minute at busy times! Late-night shifts can be stressful—you may have to deal with drunk or rude customers. The environment in the restaurant is often hot, busy, and noisy. Many fast foods, including burgers, french fries, and pizza, are unhealthy. It's fine to eat them occasionally, but consuming them regularly can be harmful. It's worth bearing this in mind, because you will probably find yourself eating the food on your breaks.

Although the flexibility of the shift patterns can be an advantage, you may have to work early mornings, and you'll be particularly in demand for shifts in the evenings, on weekends, and during holidays.

FINE-DINING SERVICE

In the fast-food industry, the emphasis is clearly on serving customers as quickly as possible. At the other end of the scale are formal restaurants for fine dining, where the service is every bit as important as the food. In a sit-down restaurant—which can range from casual to formal—waiters and waitresses bring plated meals to customers seated at a table.

TO BE A SOMMELIER, YOU WILL NEED

●

a keen interest in wine

●

a good palate, for wine tastings

●

knowledge of wines from around the world

SOMMELIERS

A sommelier (wine waiter) is the wine expert in a fine restaurant or wine bar who advises customers on the wine list. The head sommelier is in charge of buying wines, creating the wine list and cocktail menus, and managing the bar. Sommeliers travel frequently for wine tastings.

FINDING A JOB: WAIT STAFF

You don't need particular qualifications to find a job as a waiter or waitress, but it is helpful to have math skills and to know about food and beverages. Some knowledge of a foreign language may be useful. Employers will choose candidates who have an outgoing personality.

A restaurant waiter removes the bones from fish before serving it to a customer. As well as presenting the food perfectly, the waiters in a formal restaurant must attend carefully to the customers, removing dishes as soon as they are finished but never rushing the diners.

A head sommelier samples some wine. Each week he and other experts meet in the wine cellar to check the state of the wines.

Mathieu: Sommelier

"I work as a sommelier for a bistro in a top hotel. Before I entered the wine industry, I went to catering school for four years. In my final year, I specialized in wine.

"I'm responsible for everything to do with the wine. Every day, I change the wine list, check that all the glasses are clean, and make sure the wine is ready for the day's functions. At lunchtime, I serve the drinks to the diners.

"Beginning at 3 P.M. I'm in the office. I place orders, deal with invoices, and check deliveries. I also organize the wine cellar—we have 500 different wines there!

"Sometimes I organize wine tastings in the evening. We create a dinner menu to go with the wines, and I order sample bottles from suppliers. At the wine tasting, customers ask me all sorts of questions about the wines.

"The job has fantastic travel opportunities. I've been to Spain, Italy, Portugal, New Zealand, and Australia to discover new wine producers. It's important to develop a good relationship with your suppliers.

"The long hours are the downside. Then sometimes you have fussy customers who don't respect the waiters, but you always have to be polite to them. It's hard physical work, too. I regularly have to carry 200 boxes of wine down to the cellar.

"On the whole, though, if you're highly motivated and happy to spend a lot of time learning about wine, it's a great job."

TOP JOB: RESTAURANT MANAGER

The job of restaurant manager varies depending on the restaurant—in particular, whether it's an independent restaurant or one of a chain. If it's independent, you have full control of the menu, the type of food served, and the price list. In a chain restaurant such as TGIFriday's or Pizza Hut, the menu is fixed.

The advantage of working for a major chain is the clear career structure. You'll be sent to training courses, for example, to gain education in food safety and customer care, as well as business-related courses, such as ones on marketing and human resources policies. If you work in an independent establishment, there is less structure, but you'll have a large degree of control over the restaurant.

RESPONSIBILITIES AND REWARDS

You'll have several responsibilities apart from the food itself, including recruiting, managing, and motivating staff, and looking after customers. You may organize special promotions to draw people to your restaurant. In this job, you'll undoubtedly work long and late hours, but if your restaurant is successful, you'll reap the rewards—personal satisfaction and a good income.

WHERE WILL I BE?
To gain the top jobs in restaurant service, you can either start at a low level and work your way up, or earn a degree in restaurant management. This industry is full of opportunities for small businesses. With several years of experience, you could set up your own restaurant.

A restaurant owner hands out menus to customers. Knowledge of food is just one element of this job. You need excellent "people" skills and financial sense to make a success of the business.

The manager of an Asian restaurant catches up with some administration tasks.

Tung: Restaurant Manager

"I'm the manager of a family-run Asian restaurant. We serve Far-Eastern dishes from China, Japan, Vietnam, and Thailand. It's a small business, so I also work as a waiter, serve drinks, and organize the delivery of supplies. My parents and Auntie Rita set up the restaurant five years ago; they had relevant experience, but I've learned all my skills on the job.

"I've gained qualifications in health and safety, and a license to serve alcohol. I've also learned about accounting so I can manage the financial aspects of the restaurant.

"I work shifts from noon till 2 P.M. and 5:30 P.M. till 11 P.M., six days a week, so I spend a large part of my life in the restaurant. We're busiest on weekends, of course—I have eight people working for me on Friday and Saturday nights.

"It's a great job if you're sociable. I like working in a family business; it provides stability and has enabled me to acquire a range of management skills.

"If you fancy owning a restaurant, I'd advise you to gain some experience first, in the kitchen and on the restaurant floor. If you want to aim for the top job, then go for it. No matter how hard it is, it will be worthwhile."

The Beverage Industry

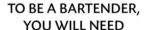

The beverage industry involves running licensed premises—bars and clubs that serve alcohol. Many pubs also serve food, so there are all the food-related jobs, too. Bars vary greatly, from locals that are part of the community to gastropubs that serve high-quality food; themed bars, such as Australian or Irish bars; and upscale, sophisticated venues. It's worth thinking about the atmosphere that would suit you.

TO BE A BARTENDER, YOU WILL NEED

●

a friendly personality

●

common sense

●

the ability to learn quickly

●

the ability to work fast at busy times

A bartender prepares cocktails. Bartenders need to know how to mix cocktails and other special drinks as well as be knowledgeable about all kinds of alcoholic and soft drinks.

A BUSY ENVIRONMENT

Bar staff are the mainstay of the beverage industry. They serve drinks, clear tables, and wash up. As a bartender, you need to be familiar with all the products, be able to cope under pressure, and above all, be friendly and welcoming to customers.

You can go straight into bar work and train on the job or take a bartending course first. If you're going to work on premises that sell alcohol, you'll need to be aware that it is important to serve alcohol safely and responsibly. Age restrictions apply for bar work. For example, in many states in the United States, you cannot legally serve alcohol until you are 18. In some states, you must be 21.

You'll be working evenings and weekends as well as daytime shifts. If you apply for bar work, do check if you'll get any weekends off. On the plus side, you'll have time off during the week.

Washing glasses and keeping the bar area clean are all part of a bartender's job.

Kathy: Bartender

"I've had a lot of experience bartending in different kinds of places. I've worked either part-time or full-time as a bartender for 25 years at restaurants, casual dining, as well as resort bars. Now, I am a co-owner of a restaurant, and I bartend there still. I started working as a bartender before I went to college and learned how much fun the job was. It's one of those jobs where you get to meet a lot of different people. One really important skill that you have to have to be a good bartender is to be able to talk with people.

"Other than being a people-person, a bartender has to be able to multitask. Some businesses will require that you attend bartending school, but most do not have that requirement. Bartending is something you really learn to do by just doing the job.

"I'm a night person, so I enjoy the hours that a bartender works. It's mostly evenings and nights because that is when most people get off work. That's when a bartender's day starts. I usually work from 4 P.M. until the bar closes at 1 A.M.

"Bartenders tend to be paid around minimum wage from the business that employs them, but, on a busy night or weekend, bartenders can easily make a lot of money from their tips."

JOINING THE CLUB

Are you a night owl? If you don't mind working late, you could consider a job in a nightclub. This can be a good area of employment for young people because it's a youthful industry. Clubs are sociable places to work. Remember, though, that the noise and crowds that might give you a rush when you are a customer will be your working environment for several hours a day. Working behind the bar is very different from being a customer. You'll also need to plan transportation home after work in the early hours.

If you want to work in a club, you should be prepared to work weekend shifts in a fast-paced environment. It can be a useful part-time job to fit around studies during the week.

TO BE A CELLAR TECHNICIAN, YOU WILL NEED

●

good manual skills

●

the ability to use tools confidently

●

the ability to work on your own

●

physical fitness

A cellar technician checks the installation of a barrel of beer. If you enjoy problem solving, this job might suit you.

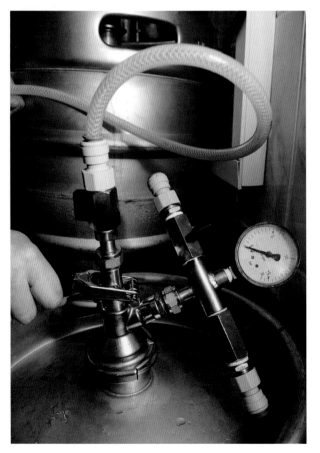

DOWN IN THE CELLAR

Bar work is not the only option in the beverage industry. You could specialize and become a sommelier (see chapter 4). If you're not so keen on customer service but are technically minded, you might like to be a cellar technician. Cellar technicians install and maintain the equipment that allows bars to serve drinks on tap. They train bar staff to use the equipment and sort out any problems that arise.

The bar equipment consists of a pump system connected to the water main, drainage system, and electricity supply. As well as understanding these systems, you'll need to use a variety of hand and power tools. It's necessary to be physically fit to lift heavy equipment, such as coolers full of water.

As a cellar technician, you'll work alone, although you need to communicate with bar staff and managers. Regarding work hours, you'll usually work a day shift, but may sometimes work evenings and weekends on rotation. You might be called in an emergency, too. You will probably work in bars over a wide area, so you'll need a driver's license and access to a car.

TRAINING

You can learn on the job but will take courses as well. There are continual developments in the industry, for example, new types of beverage coolers. You may have to attend courses to learn how the new kinds of equipment work. With experience, you can become a cellar manager.

MAIN TASKS: CELLAR TECHNICIAN

●

installing pumps and piping

●

connecting the pump system with water, electricity, and drainage

●

training bar staff to use the equipment

●

diagnosing and solving problems

●

showing staff how to use new products

TOP JOB: BAR MANAGER

A bar manager manages licensed premises. The job involves many roles, including running the venue, recruiting and training staff, setting prices, ordering stock from suppliers, accepting deliveries, and stocktaking. You're also responsible for the financial side of the business, and for organizing special promotions.

If working in a bar appeals to you, it's best to try it out before you commit yourself. Just as in clubs, working behind the bar is a world away from spending time there as a customer. Why not work evening shifts while studying during the day? If you enjoy it, you could turn bar work into a career. After a few years, it's often possible to go into management.

Alternatively, if you obtain a certificate in bar mangagement or a degree in hospitality management, you can get into the field more quickly. During your training, you'll acquire management and marketing skills. But remember that a sociable personality and relevant experience are more important than education in this industry.

DAILY WORK

On a day-to-day basis, your job will include ensuring the bar is clean and tidy, checking that drinkers are not underage, and socializing with staff and customers. You'll need to deal with any difficulties, such as refusing service to customers who have drunk too much.

A popular bar in Paris, France. To be a bar manager, you need a talent for spotting good business opportunities.

WHERE WILL I BE?
If you work for a large bar management company, you'll follow a structured program of training courses. If you work in an independent bar, your training will be more flexible. You can progress to become an assistant manager or manager relatively quickly. Then you could become self-employed and run your own bar.

TO BE A BAR MANAGER, YOU WILL NEED
●
a friendly personality
●
the ability to be firm
●
the ability to control your own alcohol drinking
●
math skills

A bar manager in Germany with two of her bar staff.

Andy: Pub Owner and Manager

"I've been running my own pub for 10 years. Before that, I owned a roofing business. I had a friend who ran a pub, and I used to help him out occasionally. I really enjoyed it, and when the opportunity arose to run another pub, I took it on. I had to gain qualifications to manage licensed premises, as well as taking courses in cellar management, first aid, and health and safety.

"When I came to this pub, the business was doing badly. I managed to turn it around, and now it's busy most evenings. We serve food, run quiz nights, and sometimes there's live music.

"Every morning, I organize the beer cellar, [accept] deliveries, and set up and clean the bar area. We open in the evenings during the week and from midday to midnight on the weekend.

"It's hard work, and I'm always on duty. Some days, I employ another manager to run the bar so I can have some time off, but if there's a problem, I have to come and sort it out. On the positive side, I like being my own boss, and it's a sociable job—I have many friends, and everyone in the neighborhood knows me. I love it, and I wouldn't do anything else."

Further Information

BOOKS

Brefere, Lisa M., Karen Eich Drummond, and Brad Barnes. *So You Want to Be a Chef? Your Guide to Culinary Careers.* John Wiley & Sons, 2009.

Chalmers, Irena. *Food Jobs: 150 Great Jobs for Culinary Students, Career Changers, and Food Lovers.* Beaufort Books, 2008.

Ferguson's Careers in Focus: Travel and Hospitality. Ferguson Publishing, 2007.

Friedberg, Adrienne. *Hospitality and Personal Care.* Ferguson Publishing, 2009.

Heigl, Jennifer. *Career Diary of a Caterer.* Garth Gardner Company, 2007.

WEB SITES

www.allculinaryschools.com
Learn what educational opportunities will prepare you for culinary jobs. This web site offers information on culinary schools as well as information on various culinary jobs from chefs to catering, restaurant management, and more.

www.bls.gov/oco
For hundreds of different types of jobs—such as those in the hospitality, food, and beverage industries—the Occupational Outlook Handbook gives information on education needed, earnings, job prospects, and more.

www.careervoyages.gov/hospitality-main.cfm
This web site, by the U.S. Department of Labor, gives a useful overview of and statistics from the hospitality industry.

www.hcareers.com
In addition to listing actual hospitality opportunities, this site offers overviews of positions in the hospitality industry, plus profiles, "a day in the life" features, and more.

www.whatsnext4me.com
This online career and resource center introduces high school students to interesting jobs and opportunities in the hospitality industry.

Glossary

abattoir   a building where animals are killed for food

bistro   a small, informal restaurant

boutique hotel   a luxurious hotel that has its own individual style, unlike large chain hotels

butler   a person who offers a personal service to hotel guests, making sure they have everything they need for a comfortable stay

cafeteria   an eating place where large numbers of people are served, for example, in a school or workplace; usually people line up for their food rather than being served by waiters

cellar technician   a person who installs and maintains bar equipment

chef de partie   the head of a section of the kitchen, producing one type of food, such as fish or vegetables

commis chef   a chef in training

concierge   a person employed in a high-quality hotel to welcome guests, book travel, provide local information, or offer other services for them

contract catering   *see* food and service management

cook-chill catering   when food is cooked and then frozen by a food service company, then transported to an establishment where it is reheated

cuisine   a style of cooking, for example, French or Chinese

delegate   to share out work among the staff

fine dining   an expensive restaurant that offers high-quality food in an elegant setting

five-star hotel   the top hotel rating—a five-star hotel has the highest-quality rooms, facilities, service, and cuisine

food and service management (FSM)   a system in which a food service company provides a catering service for an establishment

front-of-house   the part of a restaurant or hotel that is open to the public, for example, the hotel reception area or the restaurant seating area

halal   meat that has been prepared according to Muslim rules

hospitality   food, drink, or services that are provided for guests or customers

hotel management couple   a couple who run a hotel together—usually one person is in charge of the housekeeping and the other is in charge of the catering

human resources   the skills and abilities of the workforce—a human resources manager is in charge of the welfare of the staff

invoice   a list of goods that have been sold, showing the amount that must be paid for them

maître d'   the host or head waiter in a restaurant

minimum wage   the lowest wage rate that an employer can legally pay to the workers

multitasking   being able to do several things at the same time

nonprofit sector   the sector of the economy that aims to provide a service rather than make a profit

perks   something you receive as well as your wages for doing your job, for example, free meals

placement   a job, often as part of a course of study, where you get work experience

porter (hotel)   a person who helps guests with their luggage and shows them to their room

self-employed   working for yourself rather than for an employer

sommelier   the wine expert in a top restaurant

sous chef   the assistant chef, the position just below the head chef

stock   the supplies that an establishment has

stocktaking   checking the amount of supplies that an establishment has

switchboard   a telephone system for answering calls and putting them through to people

transferable skills   skills that can be learned in one job and then used in another job

vegan   a person who does not eat any animal products, such as meat, fish, milk, or eggs

vocation   a type of work that you believe is particularly suitable for you

waiter/waitress   a server who carries food directly to customers seated at a table

Index

baggage porter 8, 9
baker 28, 29
bar manager 42, 43
bartender 38, 39
beverage industry 38–43
busser 23
butcher 28
butler 12

catering 16–21
  airline 18
  hospital 16, 17
  hotel 12
  marine 18
catering management 20–21
cellar technician 41
chef 17, 18, 21, 24, 25, 26, 27
chef de partie 24
commis chef 24, 25
concierge 9
confectioner 28
conference manager 13
cook-chill catering system 16

fast food 32, 33
fast-food server 32–33
food and service management
  (FSM) 16, 20
food hygiene 23
food services manager 13

head chef 26
health and safety 23
hospitals 16, 17
hotels 8–15
housekeeper 11

kitchen assistant 18, 19, 22–23,
  27
kitchen jobs 22–29

languages 7, 34
laundry worker 11

management skills 14, 15, 20,
  21, 24, 26, 27, 37, 42, 43
math 8, 32, 34

nightclubs 40

pay 9, 19, 20, 39
perks 9
personality 7, 8, 13, 26, 30, 34,
  38, 42
pressure 33
pubs 38, 43

receptionist 8
restaurant manager 36, 37
restaurants 26, 34, 36–37
room attendant 10

school lunches 18, 19, 21
seasonal work 10, 23
service jobs 30–37
  hotel 10–11
sommelier (wine waiter) 34,
  35
sous chef 24

training 11, 14, 21, 24, 25, 32,
  36, 38, 41, 42, 43
transferable skills 21
travel 6, 34, 35

waiter/waitress 30, 31, 34
working hours 8, 9, 12, 16, 17,
  19, 20, 22, 25, 29, 31, 32, 33,
  35, 36, 37, 38, 39, 40, 41